Lord Surname

Ireland: 1600s to 1900s

From Ireland Church Records of Baptism, Marriage and Death

Comprised of Roman Catholic and Church of Ireland Records

From Counties Carlow, Cork, Kerry and Dublin City

Compiled by **Donovan Hurst**

October 11, 2011

Printed 2012

ISBN: 0985134313
ISBN-13: 978-0-9851343-1-0

Dedication

This work is dedicated to all of those that came before us and shaped our lives to make us the people that we are today.

Dedication

Table of Contents

Introduction

This is a compilation of individuals who have the surname of Lord that lived in the country of Ireland from the 1600s to the 1900s. I have placed each entry into one of four categories: Families, Individual Births/Baptisms, Individual Burials, and Individual Marriages. If a marriage entry primarily concerns an Individual Lord who is female, then I have placed that entry under the category of Individual Marriages. If a marriage entry primarily concerns an Individual Lord who is male, then I have placed that entry under the category of Families. Images of many of these listings are available at http://churchrecords.irishgenealogy.ie/churchrecords/.

To help guide the reader of this work, the format of this book is as follows:

- Main Family Entry (Husband and Wife) (Father and Mother)

    o Child of Main Family Entry, including Spouse(s) when available

        ▪ Grandchild of Main Family Entry, including Spouse(s) when available

        • Great-Grandchild of Main Family Entry, including Spouse(s) when available

(**Bolded Text**) following any entry includes any additional information such as Residence(s), Occupation(s), Signature(s), etc. when available.

Hurst

Some of the fonts used in this work symbolizes Celtic writing. The traditional letters, numbers, and punctuation marks and their Celtic counterparts are as follows:

Traditional Letters (Uppercase & Lowercase)

A a B b C c D d E f G g H h I i J j K k L l M m N n O o P p Q q R r S s T t U u V v W w X x Y y Z z

Celtic Letters (Uppercase & Lowercase)

A a B b C c D ð E e F ꝼ G g H ♭ I í J j K k L l M m

N n O o P p Q q R ʀ S s T t U u V ʋ W ꞷ X x Y y Z z

Traditional Numbers

1 2 3 4 5 6 7 8 9 10

Celtic Numbers

1 2 3 4 5 6 7 8 9 10

Traditional Punctuation

. , : ' " & - ( )

Celtic Punctuation

. , : ' " & - ( )

Parish Churches

Carlow (Church of Ireland)

Carlow Parish and Staplestown Parish.

Cork & Ross

(Roman Catholic or RC)

Bandon Parish, Bantry Parish, Caharagh Parish, Clontead Parish, Cork - South Parish, Cork - SS. Peter & Paul Parish, Courcy's Country or Ballinspittal Parish, Kinsale Parish, Rossalettiri & Kilkeraunmor (Roscarbery & Lissevard) Parish, and Timoleague Parish.

Dublin (Church of Ireland)

Harold's Cross Parish, Irishtown Parish, Milltown Parish, Molyneux Chapel Parish, Rathmines Parish, Sandford Parish, St. Andrew Parish, St. Anne Parish, St. Audoen Parish, St. Bride Parish, St. Catherine Parish, St. George Parish, St. James Parish, St. John Parish, St. Kevin Parish, St. Luke Parish, St. Mark Parish, St. Mary Parish, St. Michan Parish, St. Nicholas Within Parish, St. Nicholas Without Parish, St. Patrick Parish, St. Paul Parish, St. Peter Parish, St. Thomas Parish, St. Victor Parish, and St. Werburgh Parish.

Dublin (Roman Catholic or RC)

Harrington Street Parish, Rathfarnham Parish, Rathmines Parish, SS. Michael & John Parish, St. Andrew Parish, St. Audoen Parish, St. Catherine Parish, St. James Parish, St. Lawrence Parish, St. Mary, Donnybrook Parish, St. Mary, Haddington Road Parish, St. Mary, Pro Cathedral Parish, St. Michan Parish, and St. Nicholas Parish.

Kerry (Church of Ireland)

Dingle Parish and Killorglin Parish.

Kerry (Roman Catholic or RC)

Duagh Parish, Killarney Parish, and Valentia Parish.

Families

- Abraham Lord & Esther Ledwith

  o Mary Lord – bapt. 20 Nov 1817 (Baptism, **SS. Michael & John Parish (RC)**)

- Arthur William Lord & Jane Unknown

  o Arthur William Lord – b. 28 Jan 1827 (Baptism, **St. George Parish**)

- Arthur Lord & Jane Unknown

  o Anthony Lord – bapt. 15 Mar 1827 (Baptism, **St. Mary, Pro Cathedral Parish (RC)**)

- Benjamin Lord & Catherine Heagan – 23 Jun 1699 (Marriage, **St. Michan Parish**)

  o Margaret Lord – b. 6 Oct 1700 (Baptism, **St. John Parish**)

  o Francis Lord – b. 21 Oct 1701 (Baptism, **St. John Parish**)

  o Thomas Lord – b. 2 Sep 1703 (Baptism, **St. John Parish**), bur. 12 May 1704 (Burial, **St. John Parish**)

  o Mary Lord – b. 3 Oct 1714 (Baptism, **St. Michan Parish**)

Benjamin Lord (father):

Residence - St. Werburgh Parish - June 23, 1699

Essex Street - October 6, 1700

October 21, 1701

September 2, 1703

October 3, 1714

Occupation - Victular - October 6, 1700

October 21, 1701

September 2, 1703

- Benjamin Lord & Mary Lewis – 12 Dec 1755 (Marriage, **St. Andrew Parish**)

1

- Daniel Lord & Ellen Donovan

  o John Lord – bapt. 8 Dec 1841 (Baptism, **Courcy's Country or Ballinspittal Parish (RC)**)

- David Lord & Anne Harrly

  o Henry Lord, bapt. 4 Aug 1835 (Baptism, **St. Nicholas Parish (RC)**) & Abigail Foster – 22 Sep 1861 (Marriage, **St. Andrew Parish (RC)**)

Henry Lord(son):

  Residence - 45 William Street - September 22, 1861

  o Jane Lord – bapt. 1838 (Baptism, **St. Andrew Parish (RC)**)

  o David Lord – bapt. 1840 (Baptism, **St. Andrew Parish (RC)**)

- David Lord & Catherine Ryan – 20 Aug 1848 (Marriage, **SS. Michael & John Parish (RC)**)

- David Lord & Catherine Unknown

  o William Lord – b. 10 Jul 1761 (Baptism, **St. Luke Parish**)

- David Lord & Margaret Unknown

  o John Lord – b. 26 May 1678 (Baptism, **St. Michan Parish**)

  o Anne Lord – b. 16 Nov 1683 (Baptism, **St. Michan Parish**)

  o Rachel Lord – b. 21 Feb 1685 (Baptism, **St. Michan Parish**)

David Lord (father):

  Occupation - Taylor - May 26, 1678

  November 16, 1683

  February 21, 1685

- David Lord & Mary Unknown

  o John Lord – b. 18 Jul 1708 (Baptism, **St. Catherine Parish**)

- David Lord & Mary Unknown

  o John Lord – b. 2 Nov 1760 (Baptism, **St. Luke Parish**)

Lord Surname Ireland: 1600s to 1900s

- Darby Lord & Unknown

  - John Lord – b. 17 Mar 1680 (Baptism, **St. John Parish**)

- Edward Lord & Cassandra Hannah Unknown

  - Arrabella Lord – b. 26 Nov 1749 (Baptism, **St. Mark Parish**)

  - Samuel Arnolds Lord – b. 6 Aug 1752 (Baptism, **St. Mark Parish**)

  - Anne Hannah Lord – b. 30 Oct 1759 (Baptism, **St. Mark Parish**)

Edward Lord (father):

    Residence - Lazer's Hill - November 26, 1749

               August 6, 1752

               October 30, 1759

- Edward Lord & Ellen Casey – 17 May 1845 (Marriage, **Killarney Parish (RC)**)

Edward Lord (husband):

    Residence - Cheswick - May 17, 1845

Ellen Casey (wife):

    Residence - Killarney - May 17, 1845

- Edward Lord & Jane Madden – 16 Aug 1770 (Marriage, **St. Bride Parish**)

Edward Lord (husband):

    Residence - Bermuda - August 16, 1770

- Edward Lord & Jane Madden – 18 Aug 1770 (Marriage, **St. Peter Parish**)

- Edward Lord & Lydia Forbes – 22 Feb 1709 (Marriage, **St. Werburgh Parish**)

  - Mary Lord – b. 11 May 1711 (Baptism, **St. Werburgh Parish**), d. 13 Dec 1714 (Burial, **St. Werburgh Parish**)

  - Anne Lord – b. 29 Sep 1713 (Baptism, **St. Werburgh Parish**), d. 10 Oct 1713 (Burial, **St. Werburgh Parish**)

  - Bowlton Lord – b. 22 Jun 1715 (Baptism, **St. Werburgh Parish**)

Hurst

- John Lord – b. Jul 1716 (Baptism, **St. Werburgh Parish**)

- Edward Lord – b. 16 Nov 1718 (Baptism, **St. Werburgh Parish**)

- Dorothy Lord – b. 13 Jul 1722 (Baptism, **St. Werburgh Parish**)

- Carrol Lord – b. 1720, bapt. 19 Jul 1723 (Baptism, **St. Werburgh Parish**), d. 3 Nov 1726 (Burial,

  St. Werburgh Parish)

Carrol Lord (son):

Age at Death - 6 years

Cause of Death - consumption

- Arthur Lord – b. 29 Sep 1723 (Baptism, **St. Werburgh Parish**)

- Catherine Lord – b. 12 Oct 1724 (Baptism, **St. Werburgh Parish**), d. 22 Apr 1725 (Burial, **St.**

  Werburgh Parish)

- Mable Lord – b. 13 Jun 1726 (Baptism, **St. Werburgh Parish**)

- Mary Lord – b. 12 Jun 1727 (Baptism, **St. Werburgh Parish**)

- Madin Lord – b. 12 Jul 1729 (Baptism, **St. Werburgh Parish**)

Edward Lord (father):

Residence - Werburgh Street - May 11, 1711

September 29, 1713

June 22, 1715

July 1716

November 16, 1718

1720

July 13, 1722

September 29, 1723

October 12, 1724

June 13, 1726

June 12, 1727

July 12, 1729

Lord Surname Ireland: 1600s to 1900s

- Edward Lord & Margaret Rochford – 20 Dec 1657 (Marriage, **St. Michan Parish**)

Church Register Entry was previously transcribed as follows:

"The Banes of Matrimony were published three severall Markett dayes betweene Edward Lord and Margarett Rochford in the open Markett of Dublin betweene the hours of xi and two of the Clocke being uppon Saturdayes viztt on the 12th of Decmeber 1657 : and on the 19th and six and twentyeth dayes of the same moneth, 1657."

- Edward Lord & Unknown

  o John Lord – b. 13 Feb 1682 (Baptism, **St. Catherine Parish**)

- Edward Lord & Unknown

  o Edward Lord & Ellen Casey – 5 Jun 1845 (Marriage, **St. George Parish**)

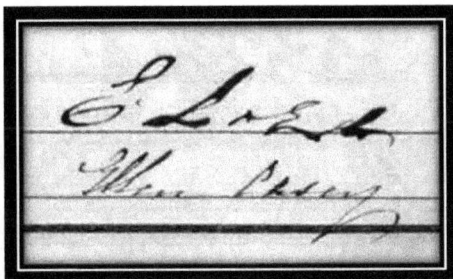

Signatures:

Edward Lord (son):

Residence - 2 St. George's Place - June 5, 1845

Occupation - Gentleman - June 5, 1845

Relationship Status at Marriage - widow

Ellen Casey, daughter of Daniel Casey (daughter-in-law):

Residence - St. George's Place - June 5, 1845

Occupation - Gentlewoman - June 5, 1845

Relationship Status at Marriage - minor age

Hurst

Daniel Casey (father):

   Occupation - Gentleman

Edward Lord (father):

   Occupation - Gentleman

- Francis Lord & Catherine Unknown

   o Gabriel Lord – b. 19 Dec 1756 (Baptism, **St. John Parish**)

   o William Lord – b. 3 Jan 1761 (Baptism, **St. John Parish**)

   o John Lord – b. 1 Jan 1764 (Baptism, **St. John Parish**)

   o Mary Anne Lord – b. 27 Jan 1765 (Baptism, **St. John Parish**)

   o Francis Lord – b. 15 Jun 1766 (Baptism, **St. John Parish**)

- Francis Lord & Sarah Eyers – 11 Dec 1739 (Marriage, **St. Andrew Parish**)

- Frederick Lord & Anne Mary Unknown

   o Evelyn Florence Lord – b. 9 Jul 1893 (Baptism, **Molyneux Chapel Parish**)

Frederick Lord (father):

   Residence - Granville Terrace - July 9, 1893

- Gedi Lord & Mary Unknown

   o Bridget Lord – bapt. 1804 (Baptism, **St. Andrew Parish (RC)**)

- George Lord & Maa Unknown

   o Maa Lord – bapt. 1800 (Baptism, **St. Andrew Parish (RC)**)

- George Lord & Mary Lyons

   o Margaret Lord – bapt. 15 May 1808 (Baptism, **SS. Michael & John Parish (RC)**)

   o Edward Lord – bapt. 27 Jan 1811 (Baptism, **SS. Michael & John Parish (RC)**)

   o Catherine Lord – bapt. 11 Jul 1813 (Baptism, **SS. Michael & John Parish (RC)**)

   o Benjamin Lord – bapt. 25 Aug 1816 (Baptism, **SS. Michael & John Parish (RC)**)

Lord Surname Ireland: 1600s to 1900s

- George Lord & Mary Unknown
  - John Lord – b. 28 Jun 1747 (Baptism, **St. Paul Parish**)
- George Lord & Unknown
  - Elizabeth Charlotte Lord & William Thomas Knight – 19 Sep 1900 (Marriage, **St. Catherine Parish**)

Signatures:

Elizabeth Charlotte Lord (daughter):

    Residence - **27 St. Albans Road South Circular Road** - September 19, 1900

William Thomas Knight, son of Wellesley John Giles Knight (son-in-law):

    Residence - **78 South Great George's Street** - September 19, 1900

    Occupation - Clerk - September 19, 1900

Wellesley John Giles Knight (father):

    Occupation - Schoolmaster

George Lord (father):

    Occupation - Schoolmaster

Wedding Witnesses:

Georgina Lord

Signature:

Hurst

- George F. Lord & Elizabeth Unknown

  - Thomas F. Lord – b. 13 Jan 1890 (Baptism, **St. Kevin Parish**)

George F. Lord (father):

Residence - 17 Bloomfield Avenue - January 13, 1890

- Gulielmo Lord & Margaret Guilfoyle

  - Sarah Anne Lord – b. 23 May 1874, bapt. 26 May 1874 (Baptism, **St. James Parish**)

Gulielmo Lord (father):

Residence - 17 Kilmainham - May 26, 1874

- Gulielmo Lord & Mary Farrell – 2 May 1826 (Marriage, **St. Michan Parish (RC)**)

  - Anne Lord & James Doyle – 18 Oct 1863 (Marriage, **Rathmines Parish (RC)**)

James Doyle, son of Malachi Doyle & Anne Unknown (son-in-law):

Residence - Bray - October 18, 1863

- Henry Lord & Bridget Unknown

  - Henry Lord – b. 21 Sep 1710 (Baptism, **St. Mary Parish**)

Henry Lord (father):

Occupation - Sentry - September 21, 1710

- Henry Lord & Ellen Unknown

  - Annabella Lord – b. 26 Jan Unclear, bapt. 23 Feb Unclear (Baptism, **St. James Parish**)

  - Honora Lord – b. 5 Jun 1884, bapt. Apr 1885 (Baptism, **St. James Parish**)

  - Mary Ellen Lord – b. 4 Feb 1887, bapt. 4 Mar 1887 (Baptism, **St. Catherine Parish**)

Henry Lord (father):

Residence - 25 Bow Lane - April 1885

8 Newport Street - March 4, 1887

Occupation - Laborer - April 1885

Clerk - March 4, 1887

Lord Surname Ireland: 1600s to 1900s

- Henry Lord & Rebecca Unknown

  o Mary Lord – b. 16 Sep 1724 (Baptism, **St. Luke Parish**)

Henry Lord (father):

Residence - Coombe - September 16, 1724

Occupation - Weaver - September 16, 1724

- Isaac Lord & Elizabeth Unknown

  o Charles Joseph Lord – bapt. 1841 (Baptism, **St. Andrew Parish (RC)**)

- Isaac Verschoyle Lord, b. 1837, d. 8 Feb 1900 (Burial, **St. George Parish**) & Hannah Unknown

  o John Loftus Lord – b. 5 Aug 1896, bapt. 17 Sep 1896 (Baptism, **St. George Parish**)

  o Elizabeth Mary Lord – b. 7 Sep 1893, bapt. 13 Oct 1897 (Baptism, **St. George Parish**)

  o William Cunningham Lord – b. 19 Jun 1898, bapt. 7 Sep 1898 (Baptism, **St. George Parish**), d. 9 Sep

     1898 (Burial, **St. George Parish**)

  o Hannah Lord – b. 21 Jul 1899, bapt. 23 Aug 1899 (Baptism, **St. George Parish**)

  o Marian Lord – b. 21 Jul 1899, bapt. 23 Aug 1899 (Baptism, **St. George Parish**)

Isaac Verschoyle Lord (father):

Residence - 9 Robert Street - September 17, 1896

October 13, 1897

September 7, 1898

August 23, 1899

6 South Brigids Road - February 8, 1900

Occupation - Clerk - September 17, 1896

October 13, 1897

September 7, 1898

August 23, 1899

- James Lord & Anne Unknown

  o Anne Lord – b. 1820 (Baptism, **Rathfarnham Parish (RC)**)

- James Lord & Catherine Bales – 11 Apr 1699 (Marriage, **St. Nicholas Without Parish**)

James Lord (husband):

    Residence - The Coombe - April 11, 1699

Catherine Bales (wife):

    Residence - The Coombe - April 11, 1699

- James Lord & Catherine Unknown

    o   Mary Lord – b. 5 Nov 1749 (Baptism, **St. Werburgh Parish**)

James Lord (father):

    Residence - Pembroke Court - November 5, 1749

- James Lord & Catherine Unknown

    o   Bridget Lord – bapt. 1829 (Baptism, **St. Andrew Parish (RC)**)

- James Lord & Catherine Unknown

    o   John Lord – b. 2 Oct 1863, bapt. 20 Oct 1863 (Baptism, **SS. Michael & John Parish (RC)**)

James Lord (father):

    Residence - 17 Fishamble Street - October 20, 1863

- James Lord & Eleanor Unknown – 8 Aug 1848 (Marriage, **St. Michan Parish (RC)**)

- James Lord & Margaret Black – 31 May 1766 (Marriage, **St. Anne Parish**)

James Lord (husband):

    Occupation - Bishop of Down and Conner - May 31, 1766

- James Lord & Mary Anne Hughes

    o   Matilda M. M. Lord – b. 11 Jun 1875, bapt. 1 Jul 1875 (Baptism, **Rathmines Parish (RC)**)

James Lord (father):

    Residence - Rathmines - July 1, 1875

- James Lord & Martha Unknown

    o   Martha Lord – b. 1 Dec 1751 (Baptism, **St. Werburgh Parish**)

James Lord (father):

    Residence - Copper Alley - December 1, 1751

Lord Surname Ireland: 1600s to 1900s

- James Lord & Mary Blake

  o Catherine Nora Lord – b. 1901, bapt. 1901 (Baptism, **St. Andrew Parish (RC)**)

James Lord (father):

Residence - 55 Queens Square - 1901

- James Lord & Mary McCarthy – 30 Jan 1853 (Marriage, **Courcy's Country or Ballinspittal Parish (RC)**)

- James Lord & Mary Unknown

  o Mary Lord – b. 1772, bapt. 24 Jun 1772 (Baptism, **St. Mary Parish**), bur. 14 Sep 1776 (Burial, **St. Mary Parish**)

Church register entry reads as follows:

"Mr. Lord's Child of Caple St."

  o Jane Lord – b. 12 Mar 1777 (Baptism, **St. Mary Parish**)

  o Frances Elizabeth Lord – b. 23 May 1778 (Baptism, **St. Mary Parish**)

  o Mary Lord – b. 12 Sep 1779 (Baptism, **St. Mary Parish**)

  o David Lord – b. 4 Nov 1779 (Baptism, **St. Mary Parish**)

  o Sarah Lord – b. 8 Jun 1782 (Baptism, **St. Mary Parish**)

  o Charlotte Lord – b. 3 Feb 1788 (Baptism, **St. Mary Parish**)

James Lord (father):

Residence - Caple Street - June 24, 1772

March 12, 1777

May 23, 1778

September 12, 1779

- James Lord & Unknown

  o William North Lord & Harriett Whitehead – 9 Sep 1878 (Marriage, **Rathmines Parish**)

Signatures:

William North Lord (son):

Residence - 27 Effra Road - September 9, 1878

Occupation - Builder - September 9, 1878

Relationship Status at Marriage - widow

Harriett Whitehead, daughter of Henry Whitehead (daughter-in-law):

Residence - 153 Rathmines Road - September 9, 1878

Henry Whitehead (father):

Occupation - Organ Builder

James Lord (father):

Occupation - Bricklayer

- James Lord & Unknown

  o Henry Thomas Lord, b. 1874 & Mary Elizabeth Whitham, b. 1868 – 28 Sep 1895 (Marriage, **Killorglin Parish**)

Henry Thomas Lord (son):

Residence - The Towers, Glenbeigh - September 28, 1895

Occupation - Bombadier - September 28, 1895

Mary Elizabeth Whitham, daughter of Benjamin Whitham (daughter-in-law):

Residence - Glennside, England - September 28, 1895

Occupation - Domestic Servant - September 28, 1895

Benjamin Whitham (father):

Occupation - File Cutter

Lord Surname Ireland: 1600s to 1900s

James Lord (father):

Occupation - Farmer

- Jerry Lord & Margaret Cummins

  ○ Joan Lord – bapt. 18 Jan 1821 (Baptism, **Courcy's Country or Ballinspittal Parish** (RC))

- John Lord & Anne McCormick – 16 Jan 1814 (Marriage, **St. Mary, Pro Cathedral Parish** (RC))

  ○ Anne Hannah Lord – bapt. 12 Dec 1814 (Baptism, **St. Mary, Pro Cathedral Parish** (RC))

  ○ Edward Lord – bapt. 10 Oct 1816 (Baptism, **St. Mary, Pro Cathedral Parish** (RC))

- John Lord & Delia Garland

  ○ Charles Verschoyle Lord, b. 4 Dec 1839, bapt. 13 Aug 1875 (Baptism, **Rathmines Parish** (RC)) & Mary Gartland – 29 Apr 1863

    ▪ Adelaide Jane M. Lord – b. 21 May 1864, bapt. 14 Jun 1864 (Baptism, **Rathmines Parish** (RC)) & James Donnelly – 23 Feb 1889 (Marriage, **Rathmines Parish** (RC))

      • Mary Adelaide Magdalen Donnelly – b. 15 Sep 1890, bapt. 21 Sep 1890 (Baptism, **Rathmines Parish** (RC))

Adelaide Jane M. Lord (daughter):

Residence - 53 Harold's Cross - February 23, 1889

James Donnelly, son of Joseph Donnelly & Catherine Sheehy (son-in-law):

Residence - 6 Shamrock Villa Harold's Cross - February 23, 1888

  ▪ Gulielmo Charles Lord – b. 18 Jul 1865, bapt. 18 Aug 1865 (Baptism, **St. Lawrence Parish** (RC))

  ▪ Mary A. P. Lord – b. 18 May 1867, bapt. 15 Aug 1867 (Baptism, **Rathmines Parish** (RC))

  ▪ John J. F. Lord – b. 18 Aug 1868, bapt. 14 May 1869 (Baptism, **Rathmines Parish** (RC))

  ▪ Samuel J. Lord – b. 22 Nov 1869, bapt. 2 Feb 1870 (Baptism, **Rathmines Parish** (RC))

  ▪ Margaret M. J. Lord – b. 14 Mar 1871, bapt. 25 Mar 1871 (Baptism, **Rathmines Parish** (RC))

  ▪ Amelia C. Lord – b. 24 Dec 1873, bapt. 13 Jan 1874 (Baptism, **Rathmines Parish** (RC))

Hurst

- Mary Delia J. Lord, b. 10 Mar 1877, bapt. 18 Mar 1877 (Baptism, **Rathmines Parish** (RC)) & Patrick Joseph Cullen – 7 Sep 1898 (Marriage, **Harrington Street Parish** (RC))

  - Margaret Mary Cullen – b. 1899, bapt. 1899 (Baptism, **St. Andrew Parish** (RC))

Mary Delia J. Lord (daughter):

Residence - 32 Charlemont Street - September 7, 1898

Patrick Joseph Cullen, son of Gerald Cullen & Mary Anne Hart (son-in-law):

Residence - 53 North King Street - September 7, 1898

Holles Street Hospital - 1899

- Honora M. J. Lord – b. 9 Jun 1880, bapt. 13 Jun 1880 (Baptism, **Rathmines Parish** (RC))

- Hannah Lord & James Redding – 29 Dec 1903 (Marriage, **Harrington Street Parish** (RC))

Hannah Lord (daughter):

Residence - 14 Curzon Street - December 29, 1903

James Redding, son of John Redding & Jane Unknown (son-in-law):

Residence - 8 Lower Mount Pleasant Avenue - December 29, 1903

Charles Verschoyle Lord (son):

Residence - Mount Pleasant - June 14 1864

St. Bridget Avenue - August 18, 1865

Harold's Cross - August 15, 1867

May 14, 1869

February 2, 1870

March 24, 1871

Dunville Avenue - January 13, 1874

Great George Street - August 13, 1875

Longwood Avenue - March 18, 1877

Victoria Street - June 13, 1880

Charles Verschoyle Lord and Mary Gartland Marriage reference:

https://familysearch.org/pal:/MM9.1.2/9SLC-1R5/p4

Lord Surname Ireland: 1600s to 1900s

o Henry Verschoyle Lord, b. 27 Nov 1842, bapt. 27 Jan 1882 (Baptism, **St. Stephen Parish**) & Julia Adelaide Wilkins – 17 Oct 1863

- William Henry Lord – b. 29 Jul 1864, bapt. 23 Nov 1864 (Baptism, **St. George Parish**)

- Anne Wilkins Lord – b. 1870, bapt. 27 Jan 1882 (Baptism, **St. Stephen Parish**)

- Julia Adelaide Lord – b. 19 Feb 1871

She married Frederick David Harris, son of David John Wellesley Pole Harris & Sophia Conroy.

Julia Adelaide Lord Birth Reference:

https://familysearch.org/pal:/MM9.1.2/93GX-XBT/p1

- John Craythorne Smyth Lord – b. 21 Feb 1872, bapt. 27 Jan 1882 (Baptism, **St. Stephen Parish**)

John Craythorne Smyth Lord Birth Reference:

https://familysearch.org/pal:/MM9.1.2/93GP-T34/p1

- Edward Lord – b. 16 Nov 1875, bapt. 5 Jan 1882 (Baptism, **St. Peter Parish**)

- Ellen Charlotte Lord – b. 16 Feb 1878, bapt. 5 Jan 1882 (Baptism, **St. Peter Parish**)

- Annabella Lord – b. 12 Mar 1882, bapt. 15 Jun 1882 (Baptism, **St. Stephen Parish**)

- Edith Lord – b. 1882, bapt. 15 Jun 1882 (Baptism, **St. Stephen Parish**)

Henry Verschoyle Lord (son):

Residence - 5 Richmond Parade - November 23, 1864

29 Holles Street - January 5, 1882

January 27, 1882

June 15, 1882

Occupation - Clerk - November 23, 1864

Accountant - January 5, 1882

January 27, 1882

June 15, 1882

Henry Verschoyle Lord and Julia Adelaide Wilkins Marriage Reference:

https://familysearch.org/pal:/MM9.1.2/9SLZ-MCT/p4

- ○ Jessie Lord & James Gaskin – 18 Jan 1878 (Marriage, **St. Peter Parish**)

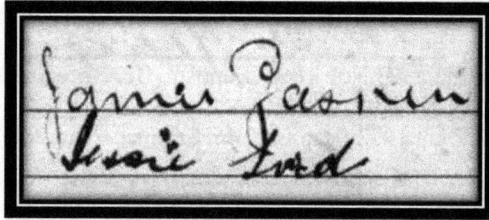

Signatures:

Jessie Lord (daughter):

   Residence - 36 Lower Clanbrassil Street - January 18, 1878

James Gaskin, son of James Gaskin (son-in-law):

   Residence - 36 Lower Clanbrassil Street - January 18, 1878

   Occupation - Clerk - January 18, 1878

   Relationship Status at Marriage - widow

James Gaskin (father):

   Occupation - Merchant

John Lord (father):

   Occupation - Coal Merchant

- John Lord & Eleanor Roe – 8 Jul 1723 (Marriage, **St. Michan Parish**)

John Lord (husband):

   Occupation - Taylor - July 8, 1723

- John Lord & Elizabeth Byrne (B y r n e)

   - ○ James Lord – bapt. 19 Jul 1837 (Baptism, **St. Nicholas Parish (RC)**)

   - ○ Margaret Byrne Lord – bapt. 24 Feb 1840 (Baptism, **St. Nicholas Parish (RC)**) & Charles Trazer –

      19 Aug 1877 (Marriage, **St. Nicholas Parish (RC)**)

Margaret Byrne Lord (daughter):

   Residence - 24 Garden Lane - August 19, 1877

Charles Trazer, son of Michael Trazer & Margaret Unknown (son-in-law):

   Residence - 24 Garden Lane - August 19, 1877

Lord Surname Ireland: 1600s to 1900s

o   James Lord – bapt. 17 Oct 1842 (Baptism, **St. Nicholas Parish (RC)**)

o   John Lord – bapt. 12 Sep 1845 (Baptism, **St. Catherine Parish**)

o   Mary Lord & John Hackett – 17 Aug 1862 (Marriage, **St. Catherine Parish (RC)**)

   ▪ Mary Hackett – b. 4 Dec 1864, bapt. 9 Dec 1864 (Baptism, **St. Catherine Parish** (RC))

   ▪ Christine Hackett – b. 1 Jun 1866, bapt. 8 Jun 1866 (Baptism, **St. Catherine Parish** (RC))

Mary Lord (daughter):

Residence - 17 Portland Street - August 17, 1862

John Hackett, son of Thomas Hackett and Margaret Shannon (son-in-law):

Residence - 119 Thomas Street - August 17, 1862

122 Thomas Street - December 9, 1864

June 8, 1866

o   Robert Lord & Anne O'Brien – 3 Oct 1859 (Marriage, **St. Catherine Parish (RC)**)

   ▪ James R. Lord & Mary Meleady – 30 Jul 1900 (Marriage, **St. Mary, Pro Cathedral Parish**

   (RC))

James R. Lord, son of Robert Lord and Anne O'Brien (son):

Residence - 22 James Street - July 30, 1900

Mary Meleady, daughter of Nicholas Meleady and Mary Flood (daughter-in-law):

Residence - 28 North Earl Street - July 30, 1900

   ▪ John Lord – b. 20 Oct 1860, bapt. 23 Oct 1860 (Baptism, **St. Catherine Parish** (RC))

   ▪ Michael Lord – b. 9 Nov 1862, bapt. 18 Nov 1862 (Baptism, **St. Catherine Parish** (RC))

   ▪ James Lord – b.10 Jan 1865, bapt. 17 Jan 1865 (Baptism, **St. Catherine Parish** (RC))

   ▪ Robert Joseph Lord – b. 9 Apr 1875, bapt. 9 Apr 1875 (Baptism, **St. James Parish** (RC))

   ▪ Gulielmo Joseph Lord – b. 8 Mar 1877, bapt. 13 Mar 1877 (Baptism, **St. James Parish** (RC))

   ▪ Anne Catherine Lord – b. 18 Oct 1879, bapt. 21 Oct 1879 (Baptism, **St. James Parish** (RC))

   ▪ Mary Teresa Lord – b. 29 Sep 1881, bapt. 2 Oct 1881 (Baptism, **St. James Parish** (RC))

Hurst

Robert Lord (son):

> Residence - 119 Thomas Street - October 3, 1859
>
> 20 Chamber Street - October 23, 1860
>
> 17 Portland Street - November 18, 1862
>
> 17 Parkland Street - January 17, 1865
>
> 22 James Street - April 9, 1875
>
> March 13, 1877
>
> October 21 1879
>
> October 2, 1881

Anne O'Brien, daughter of Michael O'Brien and Bridget Unknown (daughter-in-law):

> Residence - 10 Crane Street - October 3, 1859

- John Lord & Elizabeth Unknown

  - Edward Lord & Josephine Henderson – 8 Jul 1868 (Marriage, St. Mary, Pro Cathedral Parish

    (RC))

Edward Lord (son):

> Residence - 72 Lower Gardiner Street - July 8, 1868

Josephine Henderson, daughter of James Henderson & Mary Anne Unknown (daughter-in-law):

> Residence - 20 Summer Hill - July 8, 1868

- John Lord & Esther Winter – 4 Oct 1740 (Marriage, St. Nicholas Within Parish)

- John Lord & Hannah Unknown

  - Margaret Lord – bapt. 1 Oct 1864 (Baptism, Staplestown Parish)

John Lord (father):

> Residence - Rathcrogue - October 1, 1864
>
> Occupation - Servant - October 1, 1864

- John Lord & Margaret Berryl – 24 May 1824 (Marriage, **St. George Parish**)

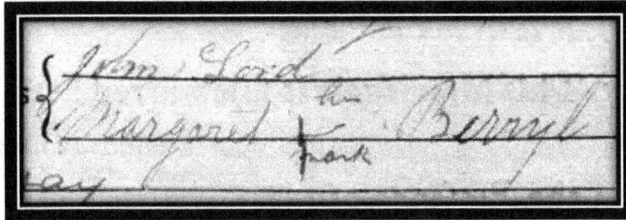

Signatures:

- o Michael Lord – bapt. 28 Nov 1834 (Baptism, **St. Nicholas Parish (RC)**)

John Lord (father):

Residence - **St. George Parish** - May 24, 1824

Margaret Berryl (mother):

Residence - **St. George Parish** - May 24, 1824

- John Lord & Margaret Keohane

  - o Michael Lord – bapt. 4 Oct 1820 (Baptism, **Courcy's Country or Ballinspittal Parish (RC)**)

- John Lord & Margaret Unknown

  - o Catherine Lord – b. 26 Apr 1780 (Baptism, **St. Catherine Parish**)

John Lord (father):

Residence - **Brethwo Street** - April 26, 1780

- John Lord & Margaret Unknown

  - o Catherine Lord – b. 8 Nov 1825 (Baptism, **St. George Parish**)

- John Lord & Margaret Unknown

  - o James Lord – bapt. 19 Jul 1824 (Baptism, **St. Mary, Pro Cathedral Parish (RC)**)

John Lord (father):

Residence - **North SD** - July 19, 1824

- John Lord & Mary Alexander – 19 Nov 1774 (Marriage, **St. James Parish**)

John Lord (husband):

Occupation - **Soldier** - November 19, 1774

- John Lord & Mary Unknown

  o Thomas Lord – b. 21 Aug 1730 (Baptism, **St. Peter Parish**)

- John Lord & Mary Unknown

  o Robert Lord – b. 15 Jul 1862, bapt. 25 Feb 1863 (Baptism, **St. Catherine Parish**)

John Lord (father):

Residence - 2 Corn Market - February 25, 1863

Occupation - Laborer - February 25, 1863

- John Lord & Mary Anne Unknown

  o James Lord – b. 8 Oct 1853 (Baptism, **St. Catherine Parish**)

John Lord (father):

Residence - Meath Street - October 8, 1853

Occupation - Drayman - October 8, 1853

- John Lord & Sarah Feltus – 25 Feb 1813 (Marriage, **Carlow Parish**)

- John Lord & Susan Priscilla Unknown

  o John Bolton Lord – b. 1 Aug 1754 (Baptism, **St. Werburgh Parish**)

John Lord (father):

Residence - Coles Alley - August 1, 1754

- John Lord & Unknown

Signature:

- Elizabeth Lord, b. 1825 & William Dugan, b. 1825 – 29 Dec 1845 (Marriage, **Carlow Parish**)

Signatures:

Elizabeth Lord (daughter):

  Residence - Carlow - December 29, 1845

  Occupation - Servant - December 29, 1845

William Dugan, son of Hugh Dugan (son-in-law):

  Residence - Carlow - December 29, 1845

  Occupation - Servant - December 29, 1845

Hugh Dugan (father):

  Occupation - Coachman

John Lord (father):

  Occupation - Servant

Wedding Witnesses:

John Lord & Thomas Lord

Signatures:

- John Lord & Unknown

  - Margaret Lord & Peter Byrne (B y r n e) – 31 May 1868 (Marriage, **St. Andrew Parish (RC)**)

    - Mary Byrne – b. 1871, bapt. 1871 (Baptism, **St. Andrew Parish (RC)**)

Margaret Lord (daughter):

Residence - 12 Fade Street - May 31, 1868

Peter Byrne, son of Peter Byrne (son-in-law):

Residence - 12 Fade Street - May 31, 1868

9 Drury Lane - 1871

- John Lord & Unknown

  - Mary Anne Lord & Michael Herity – 10 Sep 1852 (Marriage, **St. Bride Parish**)

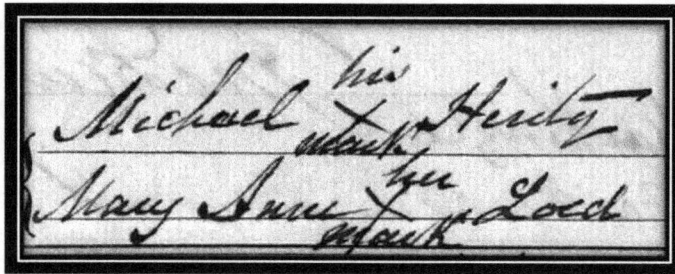

Signatures:

Mary Anne Lord (daughter):

Residence - George's Street - September 10, 1852

Occupation - Servant - September 10, 1852

Michael Herity, son of Daniel Herity (son-in-law):

Residence - George's Street - September 10, 1852

Occupation - Laborer - September 10, 1852

Daniel Herity (father):

Occupation - Laborer

John Lord (father):

Occupation - Servant

Lord Surname Ireland: 1600s to 1900s

- John Lord & Unknown

  - Ebenezer Lord & Esther Brogan – 5 Jan 1850 (Marriage, **St. Paul Parish**)

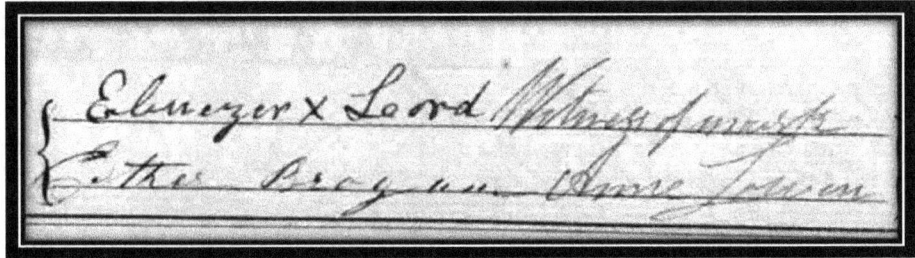

Signatures:

Ebenezer Lord (son):

    Residence - Royal Barracks - January 5, 1850

    Occupation - Private 48th Regiment - January 5, 1850

Esther Brogan, daughter of Henry Brogan (daughter-in-law):

    Residence - Barrack Street - January 5, 1850

    Relationship Status at Marriage - minor age

Henry Brogan (father):

    Occupation - Mason

John Lord (father):

    Occupation - Weaver

Wedding Witnesses:

William Brogan

Signature:

Hurst

- Joseph Lord & Elizabeth Wilson

  - Elizabeth Lord – b. 17 May 1876, bapt. 3 Jul 1876 (Baptism, **St. Nicholas Parish (RC)**)

Joseph Lord (father):

Residence - 44 Plunkett Street - July 3, 1876

- Joseph Lord & Unknown

  - Martha Jane Lord & Richard Walsh – 26 Sep 1883 (Marriage, **St. Andrew Parish (RC)**)

    - Richard Joseph Walsh – b. 1884, bapt. 1884 (Baptism, **St. Andrew Parish (RC)**)

Martha Jane Lord (daughter)

Residence - Glenpott Cottages Terenure - September 26, 1883

Richard Walsh, son of Thomas Walsh (son-in-law):

Residence - 23 Cumberland Street - September 26, 1883

8 Upper Erne Street - 1884

- Lawrence Lord & Anne Feroni – 2 Jun 1815 (Marriage, **St. Andrew Parish (RC)**)

  - Eleanor Lord – bapt. 1816 (Baptism, **St. Andrew Parish (RC)**)

  - John Lord – bapt. 1817 (Baptism, **St. Andrew Parish (RC)**)

  - Margaret Lord – bapt. 1819 (Baptism, **St. Andrew Parish (RC)**)

  - Eleanor Lord – bapt. 1823 (Baptism, **St. Andrew Parish (RC)**)

  - Cecelia Josephine Lord – bapt. 1824 (Baptism, **St. Andrew Parish (RC)**)

- Lawrence Lord, bur. 9 Oct 1799 (Burial, **St. Paul Parish**) & Jane Unknown, bur. 29 Mar 1805 (Burial, **St. Paul Parish**)

  - Elizabeth Lord – b. 1 Aug 1768 (Baptism, **St. Paul Parish**)

Lord Surname Ireland: 1600s to 1900s

- Lawrence Lord & Unknown

  o James Lord & Catherine Knight – 26 Nov 1860 (Marriage, **St. Luke Parish**)

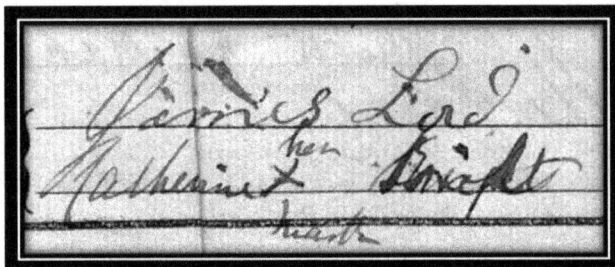

Signatures:

- Mary Catherine Lord – b. 1865, bapt. 1865 (Baptism, **St. Andrew Parish (RC)**)

James Lord (son):

Residence - 36 New Row - November 26, 1860

39 Dame Street - 1865

Occupation - Painter - November 26, 1860

Catherine Knight, daughter of Thomas Knight (daughter-in-law):

Residence - 36 New Row - November 26, 1860

Occupation - Painter - November 26, 1860

Thomas Knight (father):

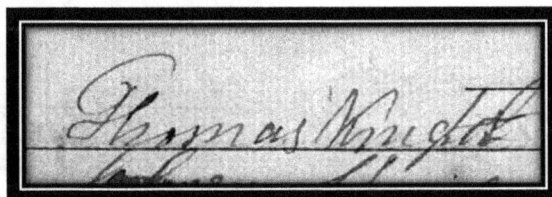

Signature:

Occupation - Glover

Lawrence Lord (father):

Occupation - Laborer

- Lodwick Lord & Unknown

  o William Lord – b. 9 May 1727 (Baptism, **St. John Parish**)

- Matthew Lord & Eleanor Unknown

  o Mary Lord – b. 27 Aug 1699 (Baptism, **St. Michan Parish**)

Matthew Lord (father):

Occupation - Merchant - August 27, 1699

- Matthew Lord & Isabel Unknown

  o William Lord – b. 24 Jan 1681 (Baptism, **St. Audoen Parish**)

  o Charity Lord – b. 15 Jul 1683 (Baptism, **St. Audoen Parish**)

  o Elizabeth Lord – b. 28 Jul 1687 (Baptism, **St. Audoen Parish**)

- Matthew Lord & Unknown

  o Hannah Lord – b. 18 May 1698 (Baptism, **St. Catherine Parish**)

- Patrick Lord & Mary Unknown

  o Richard Lord – b. 3 Sep 1754 (Baptism, **St. Michan Parish(RC)**)

- Patrick Lord & Unknown

  o Richard Lord & Catherine Wright Gilligan – 11 Nov 1890 (Marriage, **Irishtown Parish**)

Signatures:

Richard Lord (son):

　　Residence - Balrath Kells - November 11, 1890

　　Relationship Status at Marriage - widow

Catherine Wright Gilligan, daughter of Joseph Wright (daughter-in-law):

　　Residence - 1 Palmerville Terrace - November 11, 1890

　　Relationship Status at Marriage - widow

Lord Surname Ireland: 1600s to 1900s

Joseph Wright (father):

    Occupation - Farmer

Patrick Lord (father):

    Occupation - Land Steward

- Richard Lord & Mary A. Unknown

  o Ethel Mary Anne Lord – b. 27 Mar 1901, bapt. 19 May 1901 (Baptism, **Killorglin Parish**)

Richard Lord (father):

    Residence - Dooks - May, 19 1901

    Occupation - Land Steward - May, 19 1901

- Richard Lord & Unknown

  o John Lord & Honora O'Keeffe – 6 Oct 1874 (Marriage, **St. Mary Parish**)

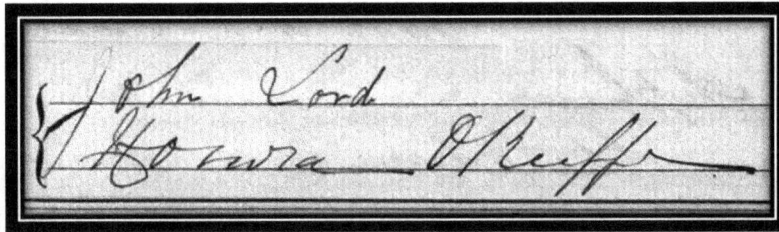

Signatures:

    ▪ Emily Lord – b. 18 Apr 1877, bapt. 19 Apr 1877 (Baptism, **Cork - South Parish** (RC))

John Lord (son):

    Residence - 76 Caple Street - October 6, 1874

    Occupation - Servant - October 6, 1874

Honora O'Keefe, daughter of Patrick O'Keefe (daughter-in-law):

    Residence - 95 Anghrim Street - October 6, 1874

Patrick O'Keefe (father):

    Occupation - Engineer

Richard Lord (father):

    Occupation - Servant

- Richard Lord & Unknown

    o Thomas Lord & Margaret Lord of 29 Hamilton Street – 1 Jun 1896 (Marriage, **St. Catherine Parish**)

Signatures:

- Constance Alicia Lord – b. 9 Mar 1897, bapt. 18 Apr 1897 (Baptism, **St. Catherine Parish**)

Thomas Lord (son):

Residence - 29 Hamilton Street - June 1, 1896

Occupation - Commercial Clerk - June 1, 1896

Margaret Lord, daughter of Thomas Lord (daughter-in-law):

Residence - 29 Hamilton Street - June 1, 1896

Wedding Witnesses:

James Lord & Jane Lord

Signatures:

- Robert Lord & Anne Dowling

    o Jane Lord – bapt. 6 Dec 1801 (Baptism, **St. Michan Parish (RC)**)

- Roger Lord & Mary Heath – 8 Feb 1705 (Marriage, **St. Andrew Parish**)

- Samuel Lord & Anne Cabe – 26 Aug 1781 (Marriage, **St. Paul Parish**)

Lord Surname Ireland: 1600s to 1900s

- Samuel Lord & Elizabeth Unknown

  o Samuel Lord – b. 30 Apr 1809 (Baptism, **St. Audoen Parish**)

- Thomas Lord & Anne Dawson

  o Christopher Lord – b. 2 Dec 1872, bapt. 9 Dec 1872 (Baptism, **St. Mary, Pro Cathedral Parish (RC)**)

Thomas Lord (father)

Residence - 3 Ward Rotunda - December 9, 1872

- Thomas Lord & Catherine Sullivan

  o Margaret Lord – bapt. 2 Jun 1770 (Baptism, **Cork - SS. Peter & Paul Parish(RC)**)

  o Cornelius (C o r n e l i u s) Lord – bapt. 31 May 1771 (Baptism, **Cork - SS. Peter & Paul Parish(RC)**)

- Thomas Lord & Frances Butler – 24 Jul 1709 (Marriage, **St. Nicholas Within Parish**)

Thomas Lord (husband):

Occupation - Barron of Canor - July 24, 1709

Frances Butler, daughter of Theobald Butler (wife).

- Thomas Lord & Frances Unknown

  o John Lord – b. 1767 (Baptism, **St. John Parish**)

- Thomas Lord & Margaret Pratt

  o Anne Mary Lord, b. 6 Jul 1867, bapt. 14 Oct 1893 (Baptism, **Rathmines Parish (RC)**) & George Bellew – 15 Oct 1893 (Marriage, **Rathmines Parish (RC)**)

Anne Mary Lord (daughter):

Residence - 18 Besborough Parade - October 15, 1893

George Bellew, son of Patrick Bellew & M. A. Doyle (son-in-law):

Residence - 18 Besborough Parade - October 15, 1893

Thomas Lord (father):

Residence - Aughtoe, Queens Co. - October 14, 1893

Hurst

- Thomas Lord & Margaret Unknown

  o Richard Pratt Lord – b. 24 Sep 1899 (Baptism, **St. Victor Parish**)

Thomas Lord (father):

Occupation - Clerk - September 24, 1899

- Thomas Lord & Margaret Unknown

  o Elizabeth Lord – b. 13 Nov 1808 (Baptism, **St. Mary Parish**)

- Thomas Lord & Mary Anne Langan

  o William Lord – bapt. 20 Jul 1836 (Baptism, **St. Nicholas Parish (RC)**)

  o Ellen Lord – bapt. 27 Feb 1839 (Baptism, **St. Nicholas Parish (RC)**)

  o Francis Lord – bapt. 1845 (Baptism, **St. Andrew Parish (RC)**)

  o Mary Lord & William Rosington – 17 Jul 1864 (Marriage, **St. Andrew Parish (RC)**)

Mary Lord (daughter):

Residence - 100 Grafton Street - July 17, 1864

William Rosington, son of William Rosington and Catherine Unknown (son-in-law):

Residence - 5 Frances Street - July 17, 1864

- Thomas Lord & Unknown

  o Margaret Lord & Thomas Lord – 1 Jun 1896 (Marriage, **St. Catherine Parish**)

Margret Lord (daughter):

Residence - 29 Hamilton Street - June 1, 1896

Thomas Lord (son-in-law):

Residence - 29 Hamilton Street - June 1, 1896

- Timothy Lord & Anne Unknown

  o Mary Anne Lord – b. 20 Feb 1803 (Baptism, **St. Mary Parish**)

- Timothy Lord & Mary Donovan

  o Cornelius (C o r n e l i u s) Lord – bapt. 14 Mar 1846 (Baptism, **Clontead Parish (RC)**)

Lord Surname Ireland: 1600s to 1900s

- Unknown Lord & Unknown

  o Leticia Lord & Paul Stuart – 13 Apr 1790 (Marriage, **St. Mary Parish**)

Paul Stuart (son-in-law):

Occupation - Gentleman - April 13, 1790

- Unknown Lord & Unknown

  o Mary Lord – b. May 1821 (Baptism, **St. Paul Parish**)

- W. Lord & Margaret Hegarty

  o Patrick Lord – bapt. 13 Mar 1859 (Baptism, **Caharagh Parish (RC)**)

W. Lord (father):

Residence - Bauravilla - March 13, 1859

- William Lord & Anne Unknown

  o Mary Lord – b. 27 Oct 1728 (Baptism, **St. Catherine Parish**)

- William Lord & Esther Unknown

  o Richard John Lord – b. 21 Apr 1861 (Baptism, **St. Werburgh Parish**)

William Lord (father):

Occupation - House Owner - April 21, 1861

- William Lord & Margaret Guilfoyle

  o David Lord & Anne Best – 24 Nov 1889 (Marriage, **St. Mary, Pro Cathedral Parish (RC)**)

    ▪ Margaret Mary Lord – b. 13 Nov 1896, bapt. 15 Nov 1896 (Baptism, **SS. Michael & John Parish**

    (RC))

David Lord (son):

Residence - 143 Upper Abbey Street - November 24, 1889

6 York Street - November 15, 1896

Anne Best, daughter of Robert Best & Margaret Smith (daughter-in-law):

Residence - 143 Upper Abbey Street - November 24, 1889

Hurst

- o Esther M. Lord – b. 3 Apr 1882, bapt. 10 Apr 1882 (Baptism, **SS. Michael & John Parish (RC)**)

William Lord (father):

Residence - 66 Lower Stephen Street - April 10, 1882

- William Lord & Mary Ennis

  - o William Lord – b. 28 Jun 1874, bapt. 3 Jul 1874 (Baptism, **St. Catherine Parish**)

William Lord (father):

Residence - Greenville Lodge - July 3, 1874

- William Lord & Mary Unknown

  - o William Lord – b. 12 Jul 1696 (Baptism, **St. Peter Parish**)

William Lord (father):

Residence - Aungier Street - July 12, 1696

Individual Births/Baptisms

None were listed

Individual Burials

- Abigail Lord – bur. 15 Jan 1709 (Burial, **St. Audoen Parish**)

- Anne Lord – bur. 1 Jun 1687 (Burial, **St. Michan Parish**)

- Anne Lord – bur. 18 Jul 1689 (Burial, **St. Catherine Parish**)

- Anne Lord – bur. 7 Feb 1808 (Burial, **St. James Parish**)

Anne Lord (deceased):

Residence - Portabella - Before February 7, 1808

- Anne Lord – b. 1783, d. 18 Jun 1817 (Burial, **St. Nicholas Without Parish**)

- Anne Mary Lord – b. 1835, d. 7 Mar 1863 (Burial, **St. Peter Parish**)

- Bartholomew Lord – bur. 14 May 1749 (Burial, **St. James Parish**)

Bartholomew Lord (deceased):

Residence - Ash Street - Before May 14, 1749

- Bridget Lord – b. 1726, d. 28 Jan 1814 (Burial, **St. Catherine Parish**)

Bridget Lord (deceased):

Residence - Brown Street - January 28, 1814

- Catherine Lord – bur. 24 Jun 1708 (Burial, **St. Audoen Parish**)

- Catherine Lord – bur.13 Feb 1720 (Burial, **St. Catherine Parish**)

- Catherine Lord – bur. 18 Sep 1805 (Burial, **St. Mark Parish**)

- David Lord – bur. 20 Aug 1770 (Burial, **St. Paul Parish**)

David Lord (deceased):

Residence - Tighe Street - Before August 20, 1770

Lord Surname Ireland: 1600s to 1900s

- Edward Lord – bur. 26 Nov 1693 (Burial, **St. Michan Parish**)

- Edward Lord – bur. 15 Apr 1788 (Burial, **St. Peter Parish**)

Edward Lord (deceased):

Residence - Kevin Street - Before April 15, 1788

- Elizabeth Lord – bur. 1 Jul 1777 (Burial, **St. Paul Parish**)

- Elizabeth Lord – bur. 19 Feb 1779 (Burial, **St. Paul Parish**)

- Elizabeth Lord – bur. 2 Jan 1800 (Burial, **St. Paul Parish**)

- Eleanor Lord – b. 1768, d. 15 Jan 1821 (Burial, **St. Mary Parish**)

Eleanor Lord (deceased):

Residence - Monks Row - January 15, 1821

- Henry Lord – bur. 23 Oct 1691 (Burial, **St. Michan Parish**)

- Henry Lord – bur. 9 May 1776 (Burial, **St. Paul Parish**)

- Isabel Lord – bur. 19 Jan 1690 (Burial, **St. Catherine Parish**)

- Isabel Lord – bur. 18 Feb 1714 (Burial, **St. Audoen Parish**)

- James Lord – bur. 27 Jun 1735 (Burial, **St. Peter Parish**)

- James Lord – b. Feb 1853, d. 13 Mar 1854 (Burial, **Irishtown Parish**)

James Lord (deceased):

Residence - Pigeon House Ft - March 13, 1854

- James Lord – b. 1853, d. 28 Apr 1865 (Burial, **St. James Parish**)

James Lord (deceased):

Residence - South Dublin Union - April 28, 1865

- Jane Lord – bur. 19 Jul 1692 (Burial, **St. Michan Parish**)

- Jane Lord – bur. 2 Jun 1745 (Burial, **St. Nicholas Without Parish**)

Hurst

- Jane Lord – bur. 24 Sep 1720 (Burial, **St. Peter Parish**)

Jane Lord (deceased):

Residence - Grafton Street - Before September 24, 1720

- John Lord – bur. 19 Sep 1692 (Burial, **St. Michan Parish**)

- John Lord – bur. 28 Apr 1695 (Burial, **St. Michan Parish**)

- John Lord – bur. 26 May 1701 (Burial, **St. Catherine Parish**)

- John Lord – bur. 18 Jul 1707 (Burial, **St. Audoen Parish**)

- John Lord – bur. 31 May 1737 (Burial, **St. Paul Parish**)

- John Lord – bur. 22 Jan 1768 (Burial, **St. Peter Parish**)

- John Lord – bur. 28 Jul 1719 (Burial, **St. Nicholas Without Parish**)

John Lord (deceased):

Residence - The Coombe - Before July 28, 1719

- John Lord – b. 1813, d. 6 Feb 1883 (Burial, **St. Catherine Parish**)

John Lord (deceased):

Residence - 44 Braithwaite Street - February 6, 1883

- John Lord – b. 1672, d. 8 Apr 1722 (Burial, **St. Werburgh Parish**)

John Lord (deceased):

Residence - Ship Street - April 8, 1722

- Lord – bur. 9 Dec 1732 (Burial, **St. Nicholas Without Parish**)

Unknown Lord (deceased):

Residence - Coombe - Before December 9, 1732

- Lord – bur. Oct 1737 (Burial, **St. Nicholas Without Parish**)

Unknown Lord (deceased):

Residence - The Coombe - Before October 1737

Lord Surname Ireland: 1600s to 1900s

- Lord – bur. 3 Aug 1738 (Burial, **St. Nicholas Without Parish**)

Unknown Lord (deceased):

   Residence - Hanover Lane - Before August 3, 1738

- Lord – bur. 24 Aug 1745 (Burial, **St. Nicholas Without Parish**)

- Lord – bur. 27 Aug 1757 (Burial, **St. Nicholas Without Parish**)

Unknown Lord (deceased):

   Residence - New Street - Before August 27, 1757

- Margaret Lord – bur. 25 Oct 1735 (Burial, **St. Peter Parish**)

- Matthew Lord – bur. 15 Oct 1684 (Burial, **St. Catherine Parish**)

- Martha Lord – bur. 28 Apr 1688 (Burial, **St. Catherine Parish**)

- Mary Lord – b. 1833, d. 15 Aug 1889 (Burial, **St. Catherine Parish**)

Mary Lord (deceased):

   Residence - 1 Brickfield Lane - August 15, 1889

- Mr. Lord's wife – bur. 25 Feb 1676 (Burial, **St. Nicholas Within Parish**)

Unknown Lord (deceased):

   Residence - Castle Street - Before February 25, 1676

- Mr. Lord – bur. 23 Dec 1798 (Burial, **St. Mary Parish**)

Unknown Lord (deceased):

   Residence - Stafford Street - Before December 23, 1798

- Mrs. Hannah Lord interred in Alderman Arundel's Tomb in the old churchyard – bur. 26 Unclear 1750

   (Burial, **St. Patrick Parish**)

Hannah Lord (deceased):

   Place of Burial - Alderman Arundel's Tomb - Unclear 26, 1750

Hurst

- Mrs. Lord – b. 1693, d. 8 Oct 1774, (Burial, **St. Nicholas Within Parish**) (Burial, **St. Nicholas Without Parish**)

Unknown Lord (deceased):

    Residence - Charles's Street - October 8, 1774

- Owen Lord – bur. 4 Apr 1708 (Burial, **St. Nicholas Without Parish**)

Owen Harris (deceased):

    Residence - Refarnum - Before April 4, 1708

- Rachel Lord – bur. 19 Dec 1686 (Burial, **St. Michan Parish**)

- Richard Lord – bur. 6 Jan 1777 (Burial, **St. Paul Parish**)

- Robert Lord – bur. 2 Jan 1818 (Burial, **St. Mary Parish**)

Robert Lord (deceased):

    Residence - Simpson's Hospital - Before January 2, 1818

- Samuel Lord – bur. 23 Jan 1758 (Burial, **St. Catherine Parish**)

- Sarah Lord – bur. 27 Jul 1701 (Burial, **St. Catherine Parish**)

- Sarah Lord – bur. 29 Oct 1719 (Burial, **St. Catherine Parish**)

- Thomas Lord – bur. 21 Jan 1676 (Burial, **St. Michan Parish**)

- Thomas Lord – bur. 3 Mar 1682 (Burial, **St. Catherine Parish**)

- Thomas Lord – bur. 3 Dec 1726 (Burial, **St. Catherine Parish**)

- Thomas Lord – bur. 24 Aug 1781 (Burial, **St. Paul Parish**)

- Thomas Lord – b. Feb 1862, d. 21 May 1862 (Burial, **St. Catherine Parish**)

Thomas Lord (deceased):

    Residence - Thomas Street - May 21, 1862

Lord Surname Ireland: 1600s to 1900s

- William Lord – bur. 16 Sep 1689 (Burial, **St. Michan Parish**)

- William Lord – bur. 25 Jul 1711 (Burial, **St. Audoen Parish**)

- William Lord – bur. 28 Mar 1733 (Burial, **St. Paul Parish**)

- William Lord – bur. 12 Sep 1741 (Burial, **St. Mark Parish**)

- William Lord – bur. 30 Sep 1707 (Burial, **St. Nicholas Without Parish**)

William Lord (deceased):

> **Residence - The Coombe - Before September 30, 1707**

- William Lord – bur. 25 Jul 1710 (Burial, **St. Audoen Parish**)

William Lord (deceased):

> **Residence - Dame Street - Before July 25, 1710**

- William Lord – bur. 16 Jun 1716 (Burial, **St. Nicholas Without Parish**)

William Lord (deceased):

> **Residence - St. Catherine's Parish - Before June 16, 1716**

Individual Marriages

- Anne Lord & Edward Allen

  - Edward Allen – bapt. 1823 (Baptism, **St. Nicholas Parish (RC)**)

- Anne Lord & John Fenwick – 17 Sep 1793 (Marriage, **Cork - SS. Peter & Paul Parish (RC)**)

- Anne Lord & John McGoghlin – 3 Sep 1811 (Marriage, **Killarney Parish (RC)**)

Anne Lord (wife):

Residence - Killarney - September 3, 1811

John McGoghlin (husband):

Residence - Killarney - September 3, 1811

- Anne Lord & Michael Nowlan

  - Thomas Nowlan – bapt. 16 Nov 1829 (Baptism, **St. Nicholas Parish (RC)**)

- Anne Lord & Patrick McCarthy – 2 Feb 1802 (Marriage, **Cork - SS. Peter & Paul Parish(RC)**)

Anne Lord (wife):

Residence - Chapel - February 2, 1802

- Anne Lord & Thomas Roarke

  - Richard Roarke – bapt. 6 Aug 1800 (Baptism, **St. Michan Parish**)

- Cassandra Lord & Daniel Keoghe – 1 Jul 1812 (Marriage, **St. Andrew Parish (RC)**)

  - James Keoghe – bapt. 1813 (Baptism, **St. Andrew Parish (RC)**)

- Catherine Lord & George Curtis

  - James Curtis – bapt. 1 May 1811 (Baptism, **St. Catherine Parish**)

- Catherine Lord & Michael Hurly

  - Michael Hurly – bapt. 8 Jul 1852 (Baptism, **Courcy's Country or Ballinspittal Parish (RC)**)

Lord Surname Ireland: 1600s to 1900s

- Catherine Lord & Matthew Cullen

  o Mary Anne Cullen – bapt. 17 Mar 1816 (Baptism, **St. Nicholas Parish (RC)**)

- Catherine Lord & Patrick Delaney

  o Elizabeth Delaney & John Doolan – 15 Aug 1865 (Marriage, **Rathmines Parish (RC)**)

Elizabeth Delaney (daughter):

Residence - Sallymount - August 15, 1865

John Doolan, son of Martin Doolan & Mary Foley (son-in-law):

Residence - Cork Street - August 15, 1865

  o Matthew Delaney & Mary Reilly – 10 Feb 1891 (Marriage, **St. Mary, Donnybrook Parish (RC)**)

Matthew Delaney (son):

Residence - Minnow Brook Terrace - February 10, 1891

Mary Reilly, daughter of John Reilly & Catharine Cullen (daughter-in-law):

Residence - 5 South James Terrace - February 10, 1891

- Catherine Lord & Patrick Leech

  o Patrick Jacob Leech – b. 27 Jan 1874, bapt. 28 Jan 1874 (Baptism, **St. Lawrence Parish (RC)**)

Patrick Leech (husband):

Residence - 5 Ralph Place - January 28, 1874

- Eleanor Lord & Edward Connallon – 27 Jan 1726 (Marriage, **St. Werburgh Parish**)

- Elizabeth Lord & Sellwood Griffin – 9 Aug 1727 (Marriage, **St. Andrew Parish**)

- Elizabeth Lord & Thomas Clarke – 16 Aug 1816 (Marriage, **St. Mary, Pro Cathedral Parish (RC)**)

- Ellen Lord & Patrick Coghlan

  o Margaret Coghlan – bapt. 6 Aug 1846 (Baptism, **Clontead Parish (RC)**)

- Ellen F. Lord & John Freeman – 8 Nov 1846 (Marriage, **St. Mary, Pro Cathedral Parish (RC)**)

Hurst

- Florence Lord & Henry John Braine

  o Henry Stephen Braine – b. 10 Jan 1895, bapt. 18 Jan 1895 (Baptism, **St. Mary, Pro Cathedral Parish (RC)**)

Henry John Braine (father):

Residence - 34 Lower Buckingham Street - January 18, 1892

- Grizelda Lord & Cornelius (C o r n e l i u s) O'Sullivan

  o Edward John O'Sullivan – b. 22 Jan 1884, bapt. 29 Jan 1884 (Baptism, **Valentia Parish (RC)**)

  o Cornelius (C o r n e l i u s) O'Sullivan – b. 13 Jul 1886, bapt. 15 Jul 1886 (Baptism, **Valentia Parish (RC)**)

  o John O'Sullivan – b.14 Apr 1889, Bapt.17 Apr 1889.

Cornelius O'Sullivan (father):

Residence - Knightstown - January 29, 1884

July 15, 1886

April 17, 1889

- Helen Lord & Gulielmo Connolly

  o Margaret Mary Connolly – b. 25 Sep 1877, bapt. 5 Oct 1877 (Baptism, **Harrington Street Parish (RC)**)

Gulielmo Connolly (father):

Residence - 32 X Kevin Street - October 5, 1877

- Helenora Lord & James Maguire

  o Michael Maguire – bapt. Oct 1816 (Baptism, **St. Nicholas Parish (RC)**)

- Isabel Lord & Samuel Fisher – 30 Dec 1770 (Marriage, **St. Andrew Parish**)

- Jane Lord & Daniel Falkiner – 23 Aug 1712 (Marriage, **St. Andrew Parish**)

- Jane Lord & Michael Hutchinson – 10 Sep 1771 (Marriage, **St. Andrew Parish**)

Lord Surname Ireland: 1600s to 1900s

- Joan Lord & Edward Doolan

  - Edward Doolan – b. 1 Jan 1863, bapt. 6 Jan 1863 (Baptism, **SS. Michael & John Parish (RC)**)

  - David Doolan – b. 1 Dec 1864, bapt. 6 Dec 1864 (Baptism, **SS. Michael & John Parish (RC)**)

  - Anne J. Doolan – b. 13 Sep 1866, bapt. 20 Sep 1866 (Baptism, **SS. Michael & John Parish (RC)**)

Edward Doolan (father):

Residence - 24 Castle Street - September 20, 1866

48 George's Street - January 6, 1863

41 High Street - December 6, 1864

- Margaret Lord & Philip Connor

  - Honora Connor – b. 18 Jun 1819, bapt. 18 Jun 1819 (Baptism, **Duagh Parish (RC)**)

  - Philip Connor – b. 8 Jun 1822, bapt. 8 Jun 1822 (Baptism, **Duagh Parish (RC)**)

- Margaret Lord & Simon Beath – 1 Aug 1719 (Marriage, **St. Werburgh Parish**)

- Margaret Lord & Timothy McCarthy – 31 Jan 1802 (Marriage, **Cork - SS. Peter & Paul Parish(RC)**)

- Margaret Lord & William Ransford – 10 Dec 1772 (Marriage, **St. Andrew Parish**)

- Mary Lord & Henry Mooney

  - Catherine Mooney – bapt. 4 May 1845 (Baptism, **St. Michan Parish (RC)**)

- Mary Lord & James McDermott (M c D e r m o t t) – 19 May 1802 (Marriage, **St. Andrew Parish (RC)**)

  - Anne McDermott – bapt. 30 Jan 1803 (Baptism, **SS. Michael & John Parish (RC)**)

- Mary Lord & John Bates

  - Henry Bates & Mary Ivory – 28 Jul 1861 (Marriage, **Rathmines Parish (RC)**)

Henry Bates (son):

Residence - Townes Street - July, 28, 1861

Mary Ivory, daughter of Richard Ivory & Christine Walsh (daughter-in-law):

Residence - Rathmines - July, 28, 1861

Hurst

- Mary Lord & Michael McGuinness

  o Gulielmo McGuinness – bapt. 29 Aug 1813 (Baptism, **St. Nicholas Parish (RC)**)

- Mary Lord & Michael Walsh

  o William Walsh – bapt. 4 Apr 1834 (Baptism, **St. Nicholas Parish (RC)**)

- Mary Lord & Thomas Murray – 23 Aug 1818 (Marriage, **St. Andrew Parish (RC)**)

  o Anne Murray – bapt. 19 Nov 1820 (Baptism, **St. Michan Parish (RC)**)

- Mary Lord & Thomas Thompson

  o Robert Thompson – b. 1851, bapt. 24 Dec 1871 (Baptism, **St. Nicholas Parish (RC)**)

Thomas Thompson (father):
> **Residence - 27 Bride Street - December 24, 1871**

- Mary Lord & Unknown Cottington – 14 Sep 1707 (Marriage, **St. Michan Parish**)

- Mary Anne Lord & Daniel Gaynor

  o Alice Gaynor – bapt. 14 Mar 1802 (Baptism, **St. Catherine Parish**)

  o James Gaynor – bapt. 29 Apr 1804 (Baptism, **St. Catherine Parish**)

- Mary Jane Lord & Unknown Toole – 1845 (Marriage, **St. Nicholas Parish (RC)**)

- May Lord & Patrick Connor

  o James Connor – bapt. 30 Jul 1851 (Baptism, **St. Michan Parish**)

- Ruth Lord & Griffin Clarke – 10 Apr 1755 (Marriage, **St. Andrew Parish**)

- Sarah Lord & William Morgan – 1 Oct 1765 (Marriage, **St. Andrew Parish**)

- Unknown Lord & William Crosby – 11 Aug 1808 (Marriage, **St. George Parish**)

Unknown Lord (wife):
> **Residence - Caple Street, St. Mary Parish - August 11, 1808**

William Crosby (husband):
> **Occupation - Esquire - August 11, 1808**

Lord Surname Ireland: 1600s to 1900s

Name Variations

Includes Latin and Abbreviated forms of names found in the original documents.

Abigail = Abuigal

Alicia = Alecia

Anne = Ann, Anna, Annae, Anne, Annie

Anthony = Anth, Anthn

Arthur = Arther, Auther

Bridget = Brigd, Brigidam, Brigid, Bridgit

Cathrine = Cath, Cathe, Catharin, Catharina, Catharinae,Catharinam, Catharine, Catherin, Catherinae

        Catherinam, Catherine, Kathrine, Katharine, Katherine

Charles = Carolus, Chas

Christine = Christina, Cristina

Daniel = Danielis, Danl

David = Dauid

Edward = Edwardus, Edwd

Eleanor = Eleonor, Elianor, Elinor, Elnr, Ellnor, Nellie, Nora

Elizabeth = Eliz, Eliza, Elizabet, Elizth, Bessie

Esther = Easther, Estre

Evelyn = Eveleen

Frances = Frans

Francis = Fran

George = Geo, Georg

Gulielmo = Gulielmus

Lord Surname Ireland: 1600s to 1900s

Hannah = Hana, Hann, Hanna

Henry = Henricus

Honor = Honora, Hanora

Isabel = Isabell, Isabella, Isabelle

James = Jacobi, Jacobum, Jacobus, Jas

Jane = Joanna, Joanne

Joan = Johanna, Johannah

John = Jno, Joannes, Joannis

Joseph = Jos

Lawrence = Laurence, Laurentti

Leticia = Letitia

Malachi = Malachy, Malichiae

Margaret = Margeret, Margarett, Margeret, Magerett, Margret, Mgt, Margt, Margtt

Martin = Martini, Martinus

Mary = Maria, Mariae, Mariam

Mary Ann = Maryann, Mary Anne, Maryanne, Marian, Mariane, Mariann, Mariannae, Marianne

Matthew = Mat, Matt, Mathew

Michael = Michaelis, Mich, Miche, Michl, Michll

Patrick = Pat, Patt, Patk, Patricii

Richard = Richd

Rosanna = Rosana, Rosanah, Rosannah

Samuel = Saml

Thomas = Thos, Ths

Timothy = Tim, Timy

William = Willm, Wm

Notes

Notes

Notes

Notes

Notes

Notes

Index

A

B

C

E

F

G

H

Lord Surname Ireland: 1600s to 1900s

I

K

L

Lord Surname Ireland: 1600s to 1900s